W9-AUI-900

Exploring the Outdoors

Kayaking

James De Medeiros

www.av2books.com

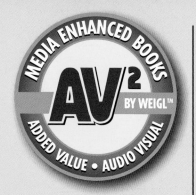

AV² provides enriched content that supplements and complements this book. Weigl's AV² books strive to create inspired learning and engage young minds in a total learning experience.

Your AV² Media Enhanced books come alive with...

Audio
Listen to sections of the book read aloud.

Key Words
Study vocabulary, and complete a matching word activity.

Video
Watch informative video clips.

Quizzes
Test your knowledge.

Embedded Weblinks
Gain additional information for research.

Slide Show
View images and captions, and prepare a presentation.

Try This!
Complete activities and hands-on experiments.

... and much, much more!

Go to **www.av2books.com**, and enter this book's unique code.

BOOK CODE

M 787749

AV² by Weigl brings you media enhanced books that support active learning.

Published by AV² by Weigl
350 5th Avenue, 59th Floor
New York, NY 10118

Website: www.av2books.com   www.weigl.com

Library of Congress Cataloging-in-Publication Data

De Medeiros, James, 1975-
Kayaking / James De Medeiros.
   p. cm. -- (Exploring the outdoors)
Includes index.
Summary: "Provides information about leisure activities that can be enjoyed in nature. Contains photos, charts, and healthy eating and exercise tips that encourage readers to get outdoors and enjoy kayaking"--Provided by publisher.
ISBN 978-1-62127-357-8 (hardcover : alk. paper) -- ISBN 978-1-62127-363-9 (softcover : alk. paper)
I. Title.
GV784.3.D4 2013
797.122'4--dc23
                    2012044677

Printed in the United States of America in North Mankato, Minnesota
1 2 3 4 5 6 7 8 9 0   17 16 15 14 13

012013
WEP301112

Project Coordinator: Alexis Roumanis
Art Director: Terry Paulhus

Every reasonable effort has been made to trace ownership and to obtain permission to reprint copyright material. The publisher would be pleased to have any errors or omissions brought to their attention so that they may be corrected in subsequent printings.

Photo Credits
Weigl acknowledges Getty Images as the primary photo supplier for this title.

CONTENTS

All About Kayaking

A kayak is a small, light boat. It has a single opening in the center called a cockpit. This is where kayakers sit. They can move and steer the kayak with a double-bladed paddle.

The Inuit are a group of Aboriginal Peoples who live in the far north. They made the first kayaks from wooden frames and animal skins. They had two types of kayaks. One was wide and had space to store items. The other kayak was long and sleek. The shape of this kayak helped the kayaker move more quickly through the water.

When kayaking in very cold waters, it is important to wear water resistant clothing.

Paddling through white waters can be challenging. It also can be dangerous.

Over time, the design of the kayak changed. People began making kayaks out of different materials. **Synthetic** material replaced animal skins. In the 1950s, **fiberglass** started to be used instead of wooden frames. In the 1980s, fiberglass frames were replaced by plastic frames. All of these changes were made to improve kayaking as a sport.

Competitive kayaking began in 1873. That year, the Royal Canoe Club of Great Britain began holding kayak races. Today, people around the world kayak for fun and for sport.

CHANGES THROUGHOUT THE YEARS				
PAST	Kayaks were used for hunting.	Kayaks were made out of wood and animal skins.	Inuit peoples wore warm clothing while kayaking.	People did not usually wear safety gear while kayaking.
PRESENT	People kayak for fun or for competition.	Kayaks are made out of plastic or fiberglass.	In cool climates, kayakers wear a wet suit.	Most kayakers wear a vest that keeps them afloat.

Getting Started

Kayaking can be a dangerous sport. It is important to be prepared with the proper equipment, including safety gear. One of the most important pieces of equipment is the kayak. There are many different types of kayaks, such as touring kayaks, folding kayaks, inflatable kayaks, and rigid kayaks.

Folding kayaks are similar to Inuit kayaks. They are made by placing fabric over a light wooden or aluminum frame. Folding kayaks can be taken apart and folded for storage. They are as sturdy as regular kayaks.

Touring kayaks are used for long-distance trips or for kayaking at sea. They are larger than many other types of kayaks. This makes them less likely to tip or turn over. Touring kayaks are made from plastic or fiberglass. They may have a place to store equipment.

Inflatable kayaks float better than many other types of kayaks. They are less likely to tip over. This is because they are filled with air. When not in use, the air can be removed from an inflatable kayak.

Rigid kayaks can absorb the impact of rocks. This makes them popular for trips down fast moving rivers with white water rapids.

All the Right Equipment

1 Double-bladed kayak paddles come in different lengths and widths. A long paddle is suited for a long kayak or tall person. A shorter paddle is suited for a shorter kayak or smaller person.

2 A helmet will protect a kayaker from hitting his or her head on objects in the water, such as rocks and logs.

3 A skirt is a piece of fabric that fits around a kayaker's waist. It attaches to the edge of the cockpit. Skirts prevent water from filling the kayak and causing it to sink.

4 Wet suits keep kayakers warm in cold water. A wet suit absorbs water. A kayaker's body heat warms up the water that the wet suit absorbs. This creates a warm layer between the kayaker and the cold water.

5 Most experienced kayakers want their kayak to have a tight cockpit space. Beginners learn better with a bigger cockpit. There are also multiple passenger kayaks that are best for families who like to kayak together. It is important to have storage space on board the kayak.

6 A personal flotation device is a jacket or vest that a kayaker wears in the water to keep afloat.

Kayaking Basics

There are many ways to paddle a kayak. As a beginner, the most important techniques are the forward, sweep, and brace strokes. The forward stroke helps the kayaker move forward. The kayaker places the right side of the paddle in the water near the front of the kayak. He or she pulls the blade toward the back of the boat. Then, the kayaker places the left side of the paddle in the water and pulls back.

Sweep strokes can turn the kayak forward or backward. This is done by placing the paddle in the water near the front of the kayak. The kayaker then sweeps the paddle out to the side and back, forming an arc in the water.

Brace strokes are especially important for beginners. Bracing keeps kayaks from tipping over. The simplest form of bracing is to keep one paddle blade underwater. High and low bracing requires kayakers to push the blade of their paddle against the flow of water. This is done by leaning forward.

Rolling a kayak takes strength, skill, and experience. This is an important skill to know before kayaking in challenging waters.

Even if a kayaker knows how to brace, kayaks can still tip over, leaving the kayaker upside down. To turn the kayak right side up, the kayaker must be able to roll the kayak. A roll is achieved when the kayaker, still in the kayak, moves his or her hips so that the body is twisted sideways. At this point, the kayaker lifts the paddle out of the water, keeping it **parallel** to the kayak. Then, the kayaker sweeps the right paddle blade away from the kayak and into the water. Holding the left elbow close to the body, the kayaker snaps his or her hips back into a straight position while sweeping, turning the kayak right side up.

Wrapping reflective tape around a paddle can prove useful. If the paddle gets lost in a fast flowing river, the reflective tape will make it easier to find.

It is important for beginners to learn paddling techniques in calm waters.

Kayaking Levels

White water, or river, kayaking is an **extreme sport**. This sport requires skill and experience. There are six levels, or classes, of difficulty for this sport. Beginners often start in the first two classes. Class One is the easiest. At this level, the water moves quickly but without any waves or **obstructions**. If the kayak rolls or tips and the kayaker falls out, the water is mild. It is easy to swim to shore. Class Two is similar to Class One, but there may be rocks in the water and slightly bigger waves.

Class Three is for experienced kayakers. It has big waves and narrow paths. Class Four has powerful waves that make paddling more difficult. Inexperienced kayakers should avoid these conditions.

River conditions can change in difficulty during different seasons. It is important to check the river conditions before each kayaking trip.

It can be useful to take a boating and water safety course before attempting to kayak in rapids.

Class Five is especially difficult and is for experts only. Rescues are difficult to perform on Class Five or higher **rapids**. These routes are known for violent and obstructed paths with very fast-flowing water.

Class Six is known for extremely dangerous conditions. It is strongly advised to avoid Class Six rapids. They are dangerous and highly unpredictable. Even expert kayakers risk serious injury by trying Class Six rapids.

River Kayaking Difficulty

Class One
no waves or obstructions

Class Two
small rocks, slightly bigger waves

Class Three
narrow paths, big waves

Class Four
difficult, powerful waves

Class Five
violent and obstructed fast-flowing waters

Class Six
extremely dangerous conditions

Staying Safe

Kayaking can be dangerous because it is hard to predict what might happen in rapids. With proper training and experience, most people learn to read the rapids for signs of danger so they can plan fun, safe trips.

To stay safe, kayakers must remain calm. They should know how to react under different circumstances, and they should build up their physical conditioning to prepare for long journeys. Kayakers who have never paddled for more than two hours at one time should not go on a four-hour trip. Kayakers cannot take breaks on the water. The only time kayakers can rest is when they have returned to shore.

One of the most important kayaking abilities is matching one's skill level to the difficulty of the rapids.

Kayakers should always check weather reports before going on a trip. It is dangerous to kayak during a storm. Waves and wind can change a Class Three rapid to a Class Six. Another risk is extreme cold. Cool temperatures and wet clothing increase the risk of **hypothermia**.

All kayakers should learn rescue skills. Accidents can happen at any time, and people should always be prepared to help themselves and anyone else in need of assistance on the water. Rescue skills include **cardiopulmonary resuscitation (CPR)** and basic first aid. Kayakers should also know kayaking signals, such as stop, help, and all is clear. To signal stop, kayakers stretch both arms out from their sides to form a horizontal line. They may also signal stop by holding a paddle above their heads in a horizontal line. Help is signaled by waving a paddle, helmet, or life vest above the head. To let others know all is clear ahead, kayakers hold one arm or a paddle straight up, high above their heads.

Kayaking Tip #2

Treat hypothermia by removing all wet clothing. Put on warm, dry clothing. Cut a hole for your head in a garbage bag, and wear the bag like a shirt. This will help reduce heat loss.

Rescue Signals

Help   Stop   All is clear

Explore the Outdoors

There are many outdoor activities that can be enjoyed on the water in addition to kayaking. Some of these activities include white water rafting, water skiing, fishing, and canoeing.

White water Rafting

In white water rafting, people travel down river rapids. The rafts are inflatable rubber boats. Often, they are steered by a professional guide who sits at the back of the raft. Many people can fit in a raft. They help the guide steer the raft.

Water Skiing

Water skiing was invented in 1922 by an 18-year-old boy named Ralph Samuelson. To water ski, the skiers have one or two skis attached to their feet, and they are pulled behind a boat. People who become very good at water skiing can take part in competitions that are held around the world.

Canoeing

Though they look like kayaks, canoes are quite different. A canoe does not have a skirt, and most canoes are built to fit more than one person. Unlike kayak paddles, canoe paddles only have a blade at one end. Most people only use canoes on calm waters with few or small waves.

Fishing

Beneath the surface of rivers, lakes, and oceans are many types of life, including fish. **Recreational** fishers use a fishing rod, line, hook, and **bait** to catch fish. Fishing can be done from the shore, from a boat, or from a kayak. Most types of fishing are not physically demanding. People of any fitness level can fish. However, fishers do need patience to enjoy this pastime.

Kayaking Around the World

1 Everglades National Park, United States
Home to more than 300 species of birds, this park is the only place in the world where alligators and crocodiles live together in nature.

2 Cyclades Islands, Greece
With more than 30 islands, including beautiful Santorini, kayakers can enjoy the warm climate while trying to spot sea life in the clear water.

3 Rock Islands, Palau
Kayakers and sport divers enjoy these 445 tiny limestone islands, which are famous for their sea caves, sunken ships, and even sunken airplanes.

4 Great Barrier Reef, Australia
The largest coral reef in the world offers kayakers the chance to see almost 1,500 kinds of fish, 16 species of sea snakes, and 215 varieties of birds.

Arctic Ocean

North America

Atlantic Ocean

1 Everglades National Park, United States

Pacific Ocean

South America

Southern Ocean

SCALE
0 — 600 miles
0 — 1,000 Kilometers

There are many places in the world where people can kayak. The best places to kayak depend on what a kayaker enjoys the most. Some places have challenging Class Six rapids. Others have beautiful natural areas. The following are a few of the places to kayak around the world.

Arctic Ocean

2 Cyclades Islands, Greece

Europe

Asia

3 Rock Islands, Palau

Africa

Pacific Ocean

Indian Ocean

4 Great Barrier Reef, Australia

Australia

Join the Club

There are many kayaking clubs around the world. No matter where a person lives, there is likely a kayaking club nearby. The U.S. state of California alone has more than 15 kayaking clubs.

Competitive kayaking is becoming more popular around the world. At the Summer Olympic Games, there are kayaking competitions for both men and women. Events include white water and flat water races. The gold medal in each competition is won by the person with the fastest time. Medals are also given for second and third place.

Many smaller competitions take place throughout the world as well. It is at these local events that kayakers sharpen their skills. These competitions help decide which kayakers will represent their countries at the Olympic Games and world championships.

Kayaking has been an Olympic sport since 1936.

Nonprofit clubs such as the American Canoe Association provide members with the latest news and events across the United States. These clubs help people meet other kayakers and attend many kayaking events each year.

Healthy Habits

Kayakers must stay fit. One of the best ways to keep in shape is to eat healthy foods. Balanced meals of grains, fruits, vegetables, dairy products, and protein will give kayakers more energy.

Grains include anything made from wheat or rice, such as bread, cereal, and pasta. All fruits and vegetables are healthy. Most nutritionists recommend eating five to ten servings of fruits or vegetables a day. A serving can be half a cup of juice or a piece of medium-sized fruit, such as a banana. People should choose low-fat dairy products, such as skim milk, low-fat cheese, or yogurt. Lean meats, such as fish or chicken, are also part of a healthy diet.

Eating cereal with skim milk and fruit is a great way to get the nutrition active people need to stay healthy.

Kayakers need energy, flexibility, and strength to paddle. Whether people want to be competitive or recreational kayakers, the more strength they have, the easier the activity will be. Flexibility allows kayakers to twist their upper body. Twisting is an essential movement for the sport. Kayakers must be able to twist in order to perform a roll that will flip upside down kayaks right side up.

Dry Land Stretches

The following exercises stretch the body in the three directions a person can move in a kayak. Try holding each stretch for 15 to 20 seconds, and repeat three times on each side.

"C" Stretch
Sit on the floor, and raise your arms above your head. Lean to the side.

Torso Twist
Sitting down, twist your chest and shoulders while keeping your lower body in place.

Leg Stretch
Lie on your back, lifting one leg straight up in the air. Grasp the leg with your hands and pull.

Brain Teasers

Test your kayaking knowledge by trying to answer these brain teasers.

Q Where does a kayaker sit?

A: A kayaker sits in the middle of the boat in an area called the cockpit.

Q What piece of equipment is used to steer the kayak?

A: The kayaker uses the paddle to move the kayak in any direction.

Q What are the three main kayaking strokes?

A: The three main kayaking strokes are the forward, sweep, and brace strokes.

Q What year did kayaking become an Olympic sport?

A: Kayaking became an Olympic sport in 1936.

Q How many classes of rapids are there?

A: There are six classes of rapids.

Q Who designed the first two types of kayaks?

A: The Inuit designed the first two types of kayaks.

Key Words

bait: food used to catch fish

barrier reef: a coral reef that runs along a shoreline but is separated from the shore by water

cardiopulmonary resuscitation (CPR): a life-saving technique that combines rescue breathing with chest compressions; used when a person stops breathing and his or her heart stops beating

extreme sport: difficult or dangerous physical activity

fiberglass: a strong material made from fine threads of glass

hypothermia: a dangerous loss of body heat caused by extremely cold weather

obstructions: objects in the water that a kayaker might hit, such as rocks and tree branches

parallel: being the same distance apart at all points

rapids: shallow parts of rivers where rocks are exposed and fast-moving water creates waves

recreational: something done for fun or relaxation, such as hobbies, games, and sports

synthetic: made by people; not natural

Index

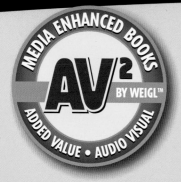

Log on to www.av2books.com

AV[2] by Weigl brings you media enhanced books that support active learning. Go to www.av2books.com, and enter the special code found on page 2 of this book. You will gain access to enriched and enhanced content that supplements and complements this book. Content includes video, audio, weblinks, quizzes, a slide show, and activities.

AV[2] Online Navigation

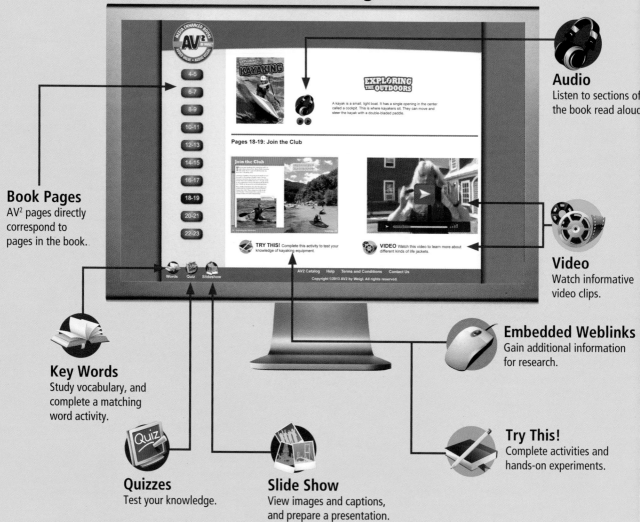

Audio
Listen to sections of the book read aloud

Book Pages
AV[2] pages directly correspond to pages in the book.

Video
Watch informative video clips.

Key Words
Study vocabulary, and complete a matching word activity.

Embedded Weblinks
Gain additional information for research.

Try This!
Complete activities and hands-on experiments.

Quizzes
Test your knowledge.

Slide Show
View images and captions, and prepare a presentation.

AV[2] was built to bridge the gap between print and digital. We encourage you to tell us what you like and what you want to see in the future.

Sign up to be an AV[2] Ambassador at www.av2books.com/ambassador.